the new house

Edition 2005

Author: Jacobo Krauel
Publisher: Carles Broto
Editorial Coordinator: Jacobo Krauel
Graphic designer & production: Pilar Chueca
Text: contributed by the architects,
edited by Amber Ockrassa and Marta Rojals

© Carles Broto i Comerma
Jonqueres, 10, 1-5
08003 Barcelona, Spain
Tel.: +34 93 301 21 99
 Fax: +34-93-301 00 21
E-mail: info@linksbooks.net
www. linksbooks.net

the new house

INTRODUCTION

There are trend setters and there are trend followers. Trend setters rewrite the old rules that trend followers then obey. It is the trend setters that we were looking for in putting together this collection. We were looking for new interpretations, fresh viewpoints, innovations. In short, we were looking for designs that are destined to determine the future of architecture. The results of our search are varied.

Since technical know-how is just as important as artistic vision in any project, we have touched upon every aspect in the design and construction processes to give a well-rounded vision.

From conception to completion, we have included information on material and construction processes in order to complement the design ideas of the contributing architects. Finally, since nobody is in a better position to comment on these projects than the designers themselves, we have included the architects' own comments and anecdotes.

Therefore, we trust that we are leaving you in good, expert hands and that this selection of some of the finest, most innovative architectural solutions in the world will serve as an endless source of inspiration. Enjoy!

Tezuka Architects / mias

Roof House

Photographs: Katsuhisa Kida

Tokyo, Japan

The clients' brief for this small house (with a total floor area of 1044 sq ft or 97 sq m) had one unconventional requirement: they wanted to make full use of the entire roof surface. When the architects first went to meet with the clients at what was their residence at the time, they were immediately shown upstairs through a small window and onto a sharply pitched roof measuring only 65 sq ft (6 sq m). "We have lunch on this roof every day," they explained. Seeing such a limited space on such a sharply pitched roof, the architects decided to not only accommodate the needs of their clients, but also to push the possibilities of their dream.

Located in the suburbs of Tokyo, the Roof House in Hadano district, Kanagawa Prefecture splits the living spaces between the ground floor and the entire roof. By maintaining a simple plan and utilizing a lightweight, yet earthquake responsive structure, the house provides a visually and tactilely generous space for the family. The thin roof, timber columns, and structural plywood panels allow for a flexible, partitioned space and open the view through the house and out toward the nearby valley and Mt. Kobo.

The partitioned spaces are also organized with eight skylights above each room, serving specific family members: the younger sister's skylight above the children's room, the elder sister's skylight above the study room, the father's skylight above the bedroom, the mother's skylight above the kitchen, and the family's skylight above the dining room. A light bulb and lantern further complement this lighting configuration to respond to nighttime activities.

Climbing up the ladders that can be propped against the ledges of each skylight, the living space extends onto the rooftop and merges with the exterior. With a freestanding wall to break the wind and provide privacy, the rooftop is equipped with a dining table, benches, a kitchen, a stove, and even a shower. The 1 to 10 pitched roof provides a comfortable and identical slope to that of the original topography and has a low roof edge to further connect the roof life to the garden life, and facilitate, for example, passing barbecue platters up from the garden. This free-flow experience and expanded usable space not only keeps the family in contact with nature, but enriches life indoors.

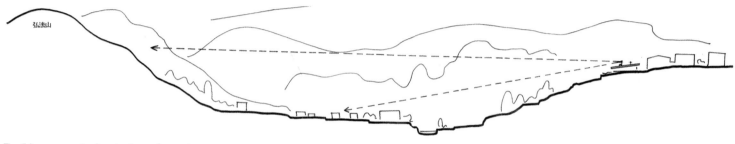

弘法山

The living space extends onto the rooftop and merges with the exterior. With a freestanding wall to break the wind and provide privacy, the rooftop is equipped with a dining table, benches, a kitchen, a stove, and even a shower.

1. Skylights to keep the entrance hall bright
2. Mothers skylight to bring up the food from the kitchen
3. Roof-top shower
4. Roof-top kitchen
5. Fathers skylight to climb up from the main bed rooms
6. Older sister's skylight to climb up from the study room
7. Younger sister's skylight to climb up from children's room

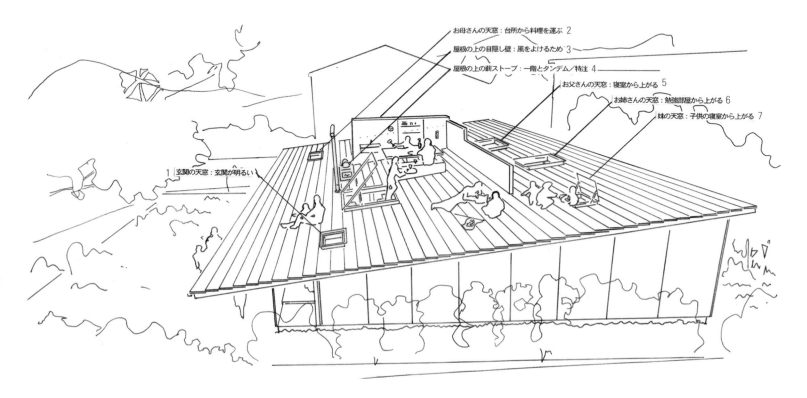

お母さんの天窓：台所から料理を運ぶ 2
屋根の上の目隠し壁：風をよけるため 3
屋根の上の薪ストーブ：一階とタンデム／特注 4
お父さんの天窓：寝室から上がる 5
お姉さんの天窓：勉強部屋から上がる 6
妹の天窓：子供の寝室から上がる 7
1 玄関の天窓：玄関が明るい

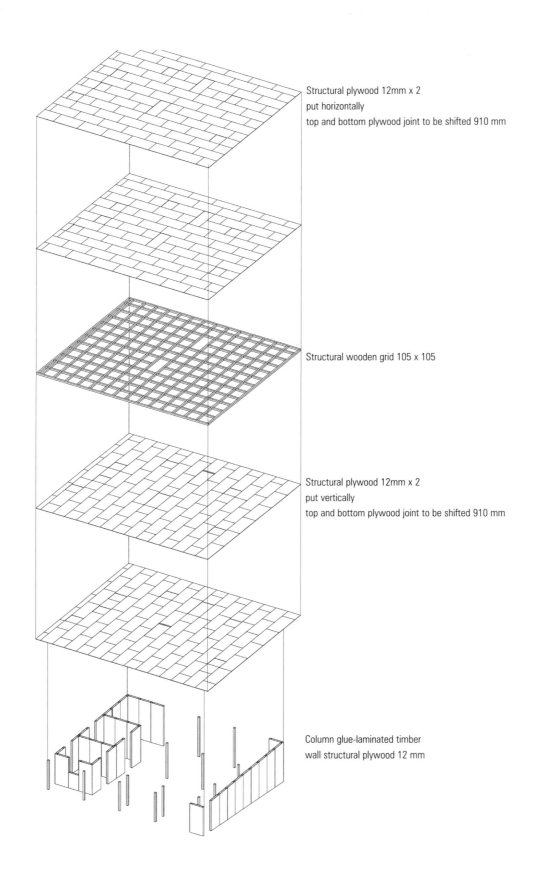

Structural plywood 12mm x 2
put horizontally
top and bottom plywood joint to be shifted 910 mm

Structural wooden grid 105 x 105

Structural plywood 12mm x 2
put vertically
top and bottom plywood joint to be shifted 910 mm

Column glue-laminated timber
wall structural plywood 12 mm

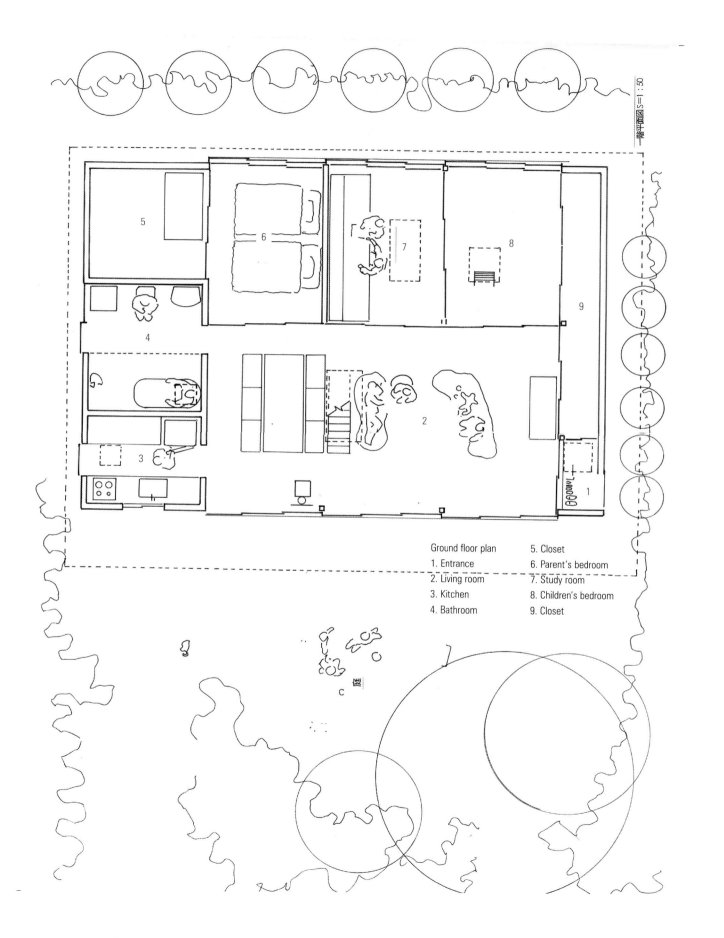

一階平面図 S＝1：50

Ground floor plan   5. Closet
1. Entrance   6. Parent's bedroom
2. Living room   7. Study room
3. Kitchen   8. Children's bedroom
4. Bathroom   9. Closet

庭

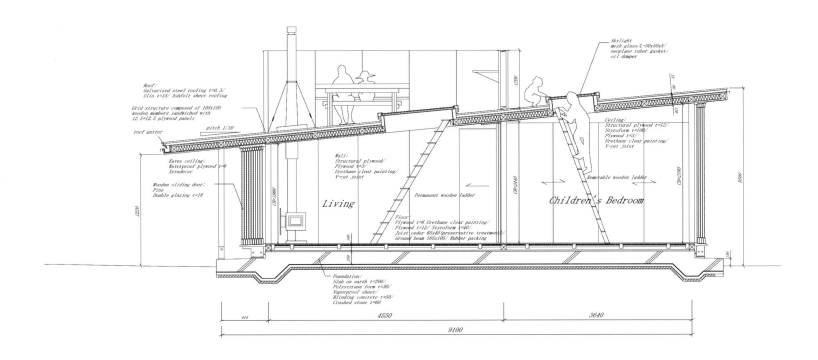

Skylight:
mesh glass/L-50x50x5/
neoplane ruber gasket/
oil dumper

Roof:
Galvarized steel roofing t=0.3/
Ulin t=15/ Ashfelt sheet roofing

Grid structure composed of 105x105
wooden members sandwiched with
12.5+12.5 plywood panels

roof gutter   pitch 1/10

Eaves ceiling:
Waterproof plywood t=6
Xyradecor

Wooden sliding door:
Pine
Double glazing t=18

Wall:
Structural plywood/
Plywood t=3/
Urethane clear painting/
V-cut joint

Ceiling:
Structural plywood t=12/
Styrofoam t=100/
Plywood t=3/
Urethane clear painting/
V-cut joint

Removable wooden ladder

Permanent wooden ladder

Living

Children's Bedroom

Floor:
Plywood t=6 Urethane clear painting/
Plywood t=12/ Styroform t=40/
Joist ceder 65x45(preservative treatment)/
Ground beam 105x105/ Rubber packing

Foundation:
Slab on earth t=200/
Polystyrene form t=30/
Vaporproof sheet/
Blinding concrete t=50/
Crushed stone t=60

910   4550   3640
            9100

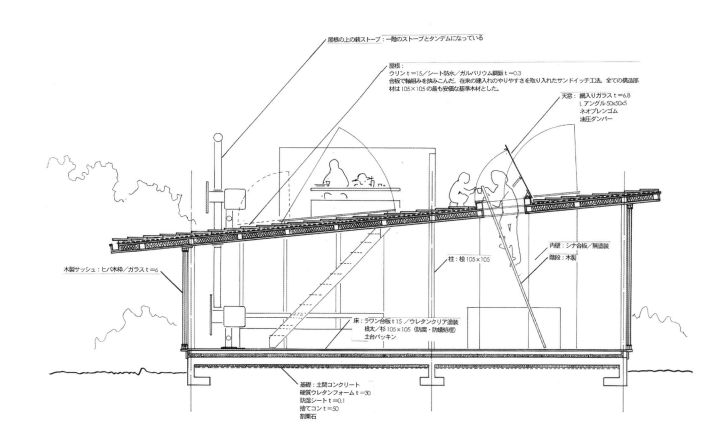

屋根の上の薪ストーブ：一階のストーブとタンデムになっている

屋根：
ウリン t＝15／シート防水／ガルバリウム鋼鈑 t＝0.3
合板で軸組みを挟みこんだ、在来の建入れのやりやすさを取り入れたサンドイッチ工法。全ての構造部
材は105×105の最も安価な基準木材とした。

天窓：網入りガラス t＝6.8
     Lアングル50x50x5
     ネオプレンゴム
     油圧ダンパー

木製サッシ：ヒバ木枠／ガラス t＝6

柱：桧105×105

内壁：シナ合板／無塗装
階段：木製

床：ラワン合板 t15／ウレタンクリア塗装
根太／杉105×105（防腐・防蟻処理）
土台パッキン

基礎：土間コンクリート
硬質ウレタンフォーム t＝30
防湿シート t＝0.1
捨てコン t＝50
割栗石

By maintaining a simple plan and utilizing a light-weight, yet earthquake responsive structure, the house provides a visually and tactilely generous space for the family. The thin roof, timber columns, and structural plywood panels allow for a flexible, partitioned space.

Jyrki Tasa

Moby Dick House

Photographs: Jyrki Tasa, Jussi Tianen

Espoo, Finland

This biomorphic house designed for a family of four is perched on a base of massive natural rocks. A stairway built from stone and a steel bridge lead to the main entrance on the first floor above ground level. One enters the building, which has a surface area of approximately 6135 sq ft (570 sq m) through an organically-shaped, stark white outer wall. On this floor there is a living-room (with a steel fireplace clad in brushed aluminum plates), a library, master bedroom and two balconies. The ground floor houses the children's spaces, a guestroom and a garage. The basement contains sauna facilities, a fireplace and a gym.

The various spaces are alternately connected via three translucent bridges made of glass and steel. Changes in level are joined by an impressive double-height winter garden and a tall spiraling staircase, which features a steel shell with oak steps and a tubular steel handrail with steel wires. This staircase, which forms the spatial core of the house, is lit by a large skylight. From the staircase one has a view in all directions of the house - either directly or through diverse glass walls.

The organically-shaped ceiling on the first floor complements the free-form spatial organization suggested by the curved white outer wall. All interior walls are rectangular in section, as opposed to the outer shell, which forms a dynamic contrast between the two. Large windows expose the house to views toward the southwest and the garden in order to capture the best light in the winter. The house's energy system is complemented by underfloor heating.

The structural framework of the house consists of concrete-filled steel pillars and composite slabs of concrete and steel combined with a roof construction in steel and wood. The facades are mostly clad in plywood, along with pine slats and boards. The undulating first-floor ceiling consists of overlapping birch veneer plates, making it possible to cover the organic form bending in two directions.

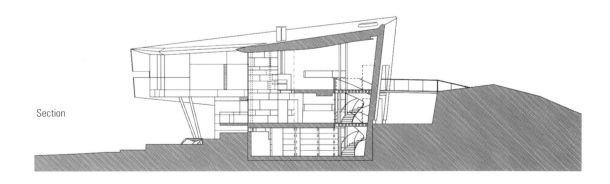

Section

The various spaces are alternately connected via three translucent bridges made of glass and steel. Changes in level are joined by an impressive double-height winter garden and a tall spiraling staircase, which features a steel shell with oak steps and a tubular steel handrail with steel wires. This staircase, which forms the spatial core of the house, is lit by a large skylight.

Site plan

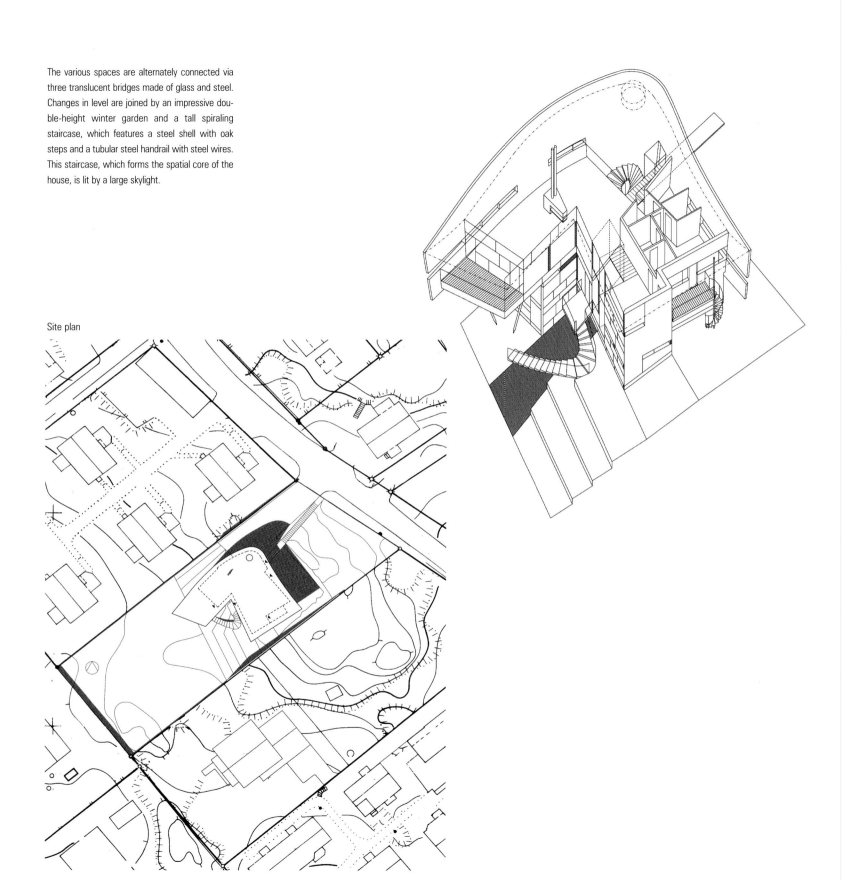

24

© Jussi Tianen

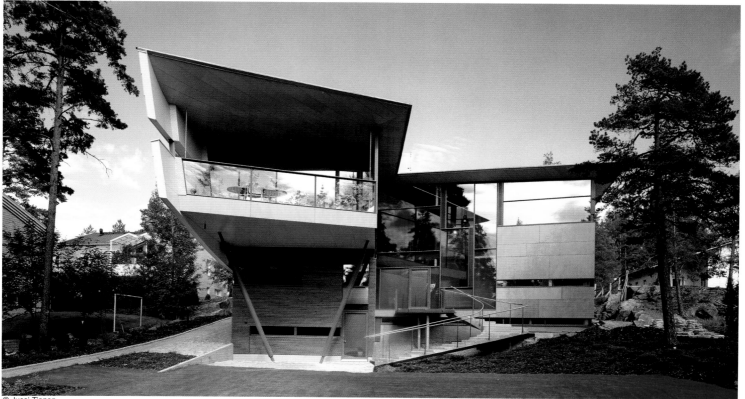
© Jussi Tianen

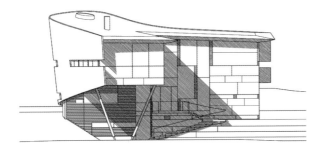

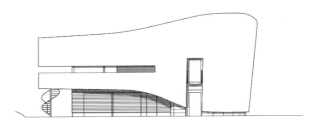

© Jussi Tianen

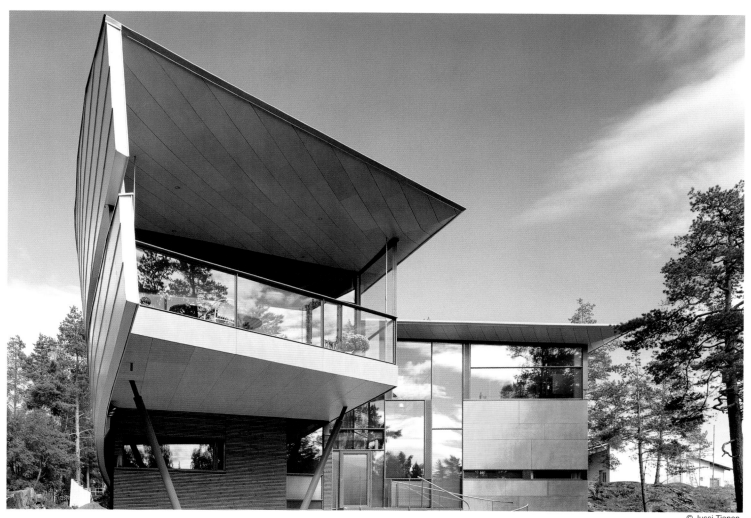

© Jussi Tianen

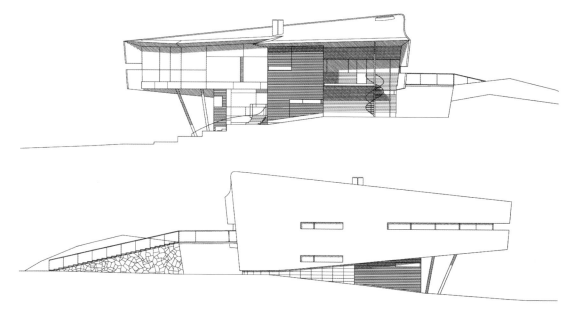

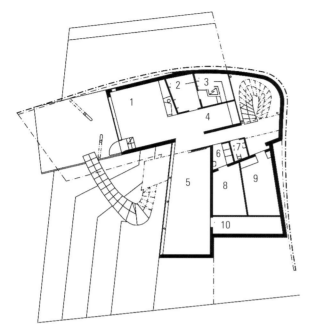

Basement floor plan

1. Sauna cabinet
2. Bathroom
3. Sauna
4. Dressing room
5. Gym
6. Cleaning room
7. Toilet
8. Technical equipment
9. Wine cellar
10. Storage
11. Bedroom
12. Clothes store
13. Bedroom
14. Winter garden
15. Hall
16. Garage
17. Terrace
18. Study
19. Living room
20. Clothes
21. Kitchen
22. Utility room
23. Balcony

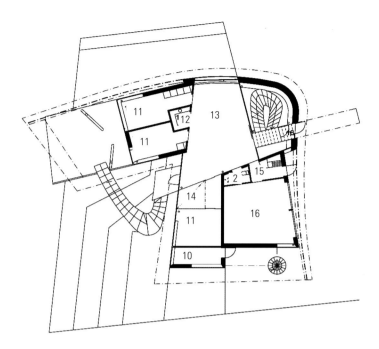

Ground floor plan

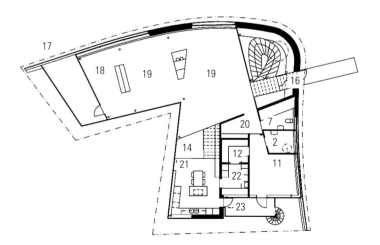

First floor plan

© Jussi Tianen

© Jussi Tianen

© Jussi Tianen

Mathias Klotz

Casa Ponce

Photographs: Roland Halbe / Artur

Buenos Aires, Argentina

Casa Ponce, with a built surface of 6135 sq ft (570 sq m), is the result of a client brief for a single-family house in a neighborhood filled mostly with 1940s-era structures in the city of Buenos Aires. The plot was extremely long and narrow (52 X 394 ft. - 16 X 120 m.) with considerable vegetation at the borders, a steep slope and views of Rio de la Plata at one end, giving the terrain a gorge-like aspect.

The aim was to keep the river-facing views unobstructed while at the same time ensuring that the house did not end up wedged in the center of the site, dividing the terrain into a distinct front and back.

The end result is a program featuring two floating volumes and a half-underground basement. The social spaces, kitchen, terraces and swimming pool are all located on the main floor, which is an entirely glazed volume that is thus visually connected to the exterior on all sides.

The upper floor is a more enclosed volume than the first; nonetheless, the bedrooms here open onto a terrace, which in turn forms part of the roof of the floor below.

The storage space, laundry, technical equipment and service quarters are located in the basement.

The construction system used was reinforced concrete. Exterior fittings are done primarily in stainless steel, while the interiors are either exposed or whitewashed concrete.

The house is a successful response to a challenging site and creates a visual interplay between volumetrics and structure. Thus, the massive unit containing the bedrooms rests on a glass volume, which in turn is seemingly suspended over a sunken base that contains the service core. Casa Ponce suggests a series of new vantage points over Rio de la Plata on a narrow site with a limited amount of sunlight.

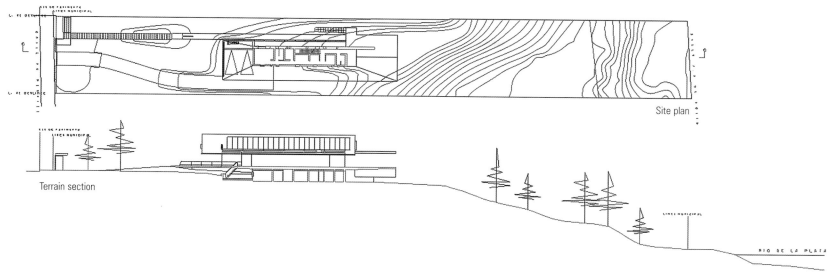

Site plan

Terrain section

The construction system used was reinforced concrete. Exterior fittings are done primarily in stainless steel, while the interiors are either exposed or whitewashed concrete.

The house is a successful response to a challenging site and creates a visual interplay between volumetrics and structure. Thus, the massive unit containing the bedrooms rests on a glass volume, which in turn is seemingly suspended over a sunken base that contains the service core.

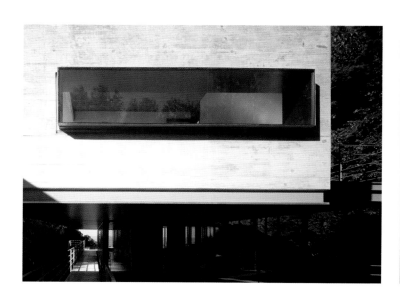

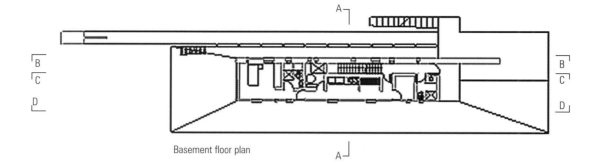

Basement floor plan

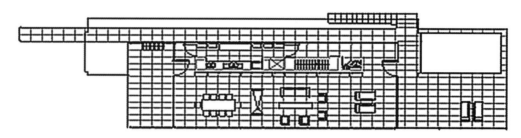

Ground floor plan

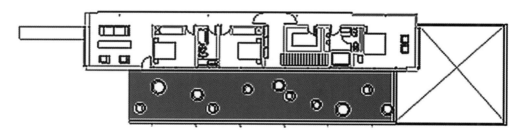

First floor plan

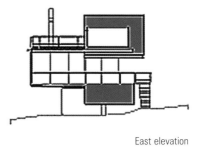

East elevation

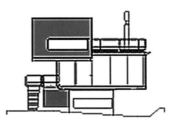

West elevation

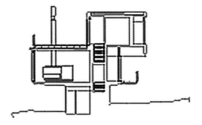

Section AA

47

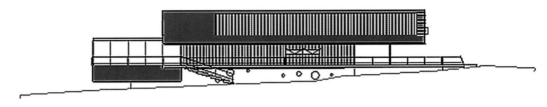

North elevation

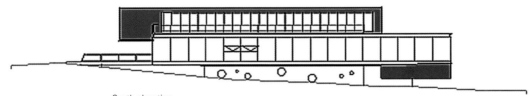

South elevation

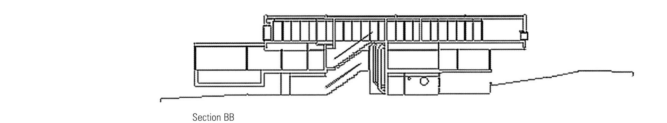

Section BB

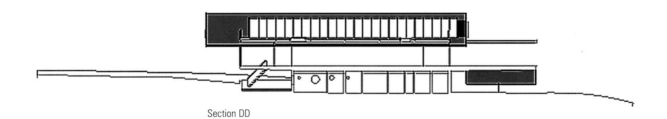

Section DD

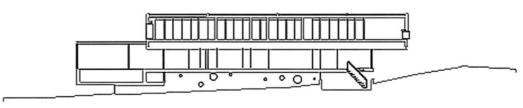

Section CC

The upper floor is a more enclosed volume than the first; nonetheless, the bedrooms here open onto a terrace, which in turn forms part of the roof of the floor below.

Arturo Frediani

Garriga Poch House

Photographs: Eugeni Pons, Ramón Prat, Arturo Frediani

Lles de Cerdanya, Spain

For this single-family house in the mountains, the designers wanted to keep the architectural dialogue as far removed as possible from the issues that so obsessed the authors of local building laws. Instead, they sought their own freedom of movement within the allowable margins.

While viewing the more specific paragraphs governing material use with reticence, the architects had no objection to the extensive application of those already used throughout the town: wood, Arabian tile and stone. The only condition that they imposed was that materials should be subject to direct use at all times (as opposed to a merely token cover-up), whether via technological or traditional methods.

The only two original walls that were still standing were worked into the new program. Their 28 inches (70 cm) of thickness, stone structure and load-bearing capabilities were used as the pattern on which the new walls would be built. The steel structure and wooden framework of the facades was inspired on the construction principles of a Steinway & Sons grand piano. The metal structure was introduced in order to ensure the dimensional stability of the wooden elements as the building ages.

The floor plan, in the shape of an eight, is split into two distinct sections joined by a 6½ -foot-wide (2 m) neck. The main section is a fully-equipped apartment with the master bedroom. The other can be used as an independent dwelling with the installation of kitchen fittings. When separated, the stairwells of each section enable independent access to the top floor.

The clients requested the maximum fluidity between the interior of the ground floor and the garden. Although openings in traditional houses in this region are generally quite small, only rarely exceeding 4 feet (1.2 meters) in width, the laws concerning windows do not limit their size along the south-facing facades. Fortunately, it was not specified anywhere how they should open; it was thus assumed that the enclosure could be a shutter-like element.

Such sizing, as well as the proportions of the other ground floor windows, presented considerable challenges in carrying out the project according to a traditional system. The demands of the client thereby depended on the applicability of a system capable of manually moving shutters of up to 75 sq ft (7 sq m) and weighing some 288 lbs (130 kg) with ease.

After working on a system using the fittings of the sliding door of a van, and subsequently abandoning the idea (they thought the bearings might eventually stick with ice), the architects used the doors on the luggage compartments of a bus as the basis for a new system. However, in contrast to their source of inspiration, their design is free of guide tracks and features two pendulum-like arms instead of just one. The shutters are thus supported at two points and balanced by a third. A prototype measuring 14 square inches (35 sq cm) in surface area with 16-inch-long (40 cm) arms was perfected in the workshop. Having achieved satisfactory results, a life-sized model that multiplied the size by 20 and the arm by 4 was put to the test.

Site plan

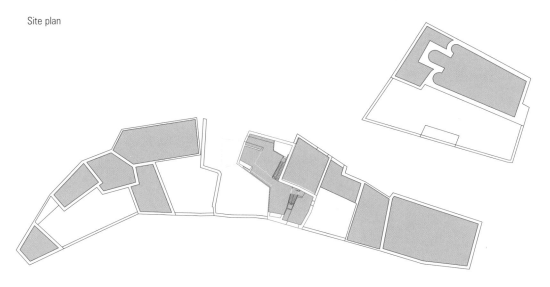

The floor plan, in the shape of an eight, is split into two distinct sections joined by a 6½ -foot-wide (2 m) neck. The main section is a fully-equipped apartment with the master bedroom. The other can be used as an independent dwelling with the installation of kitchen fittings. When separated, the stairwells of each section enable independent access to the top floor.

© Arturo Frediani

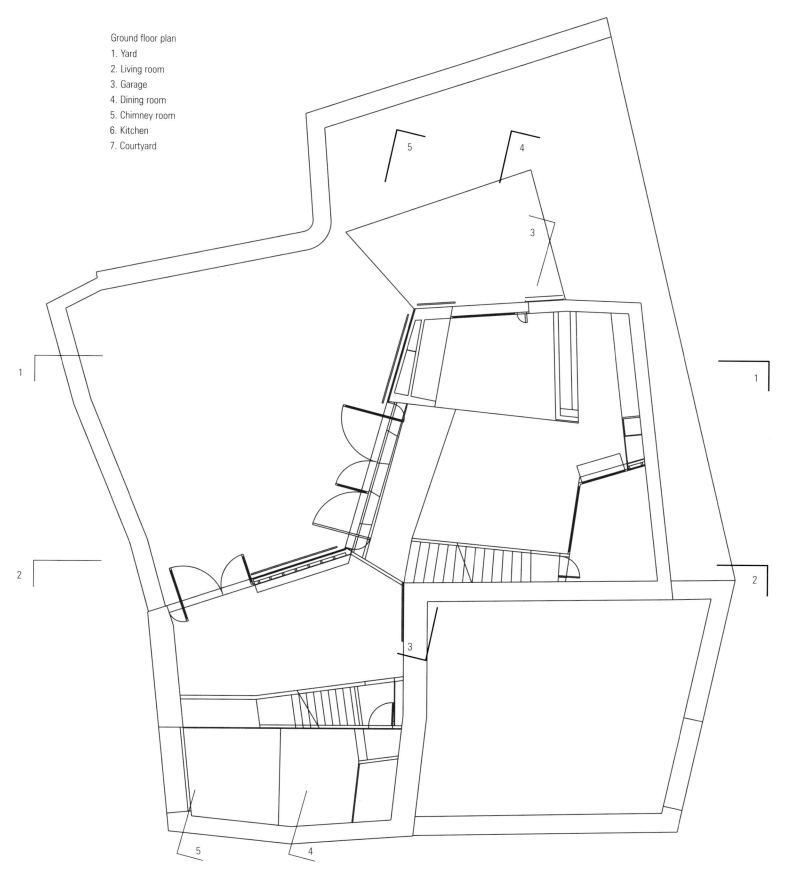

Ground floor plan
1. Yard
2. Living room
3. Garage
4. Dining room
5. Chimney room
6. Kitchen
7. Courtyard

53

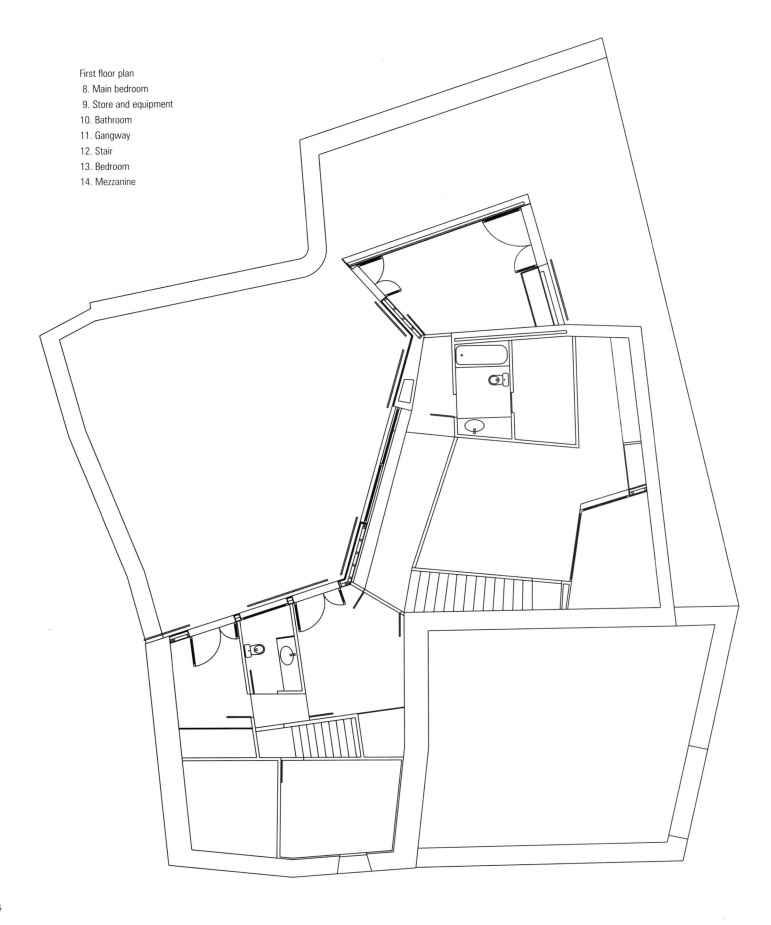

First floor plan
 8. Main bedroom
 9. Store and equipment
10. Bathroom
11. Gangway
12. Stair
13. Bedroom
14. Mezzanine

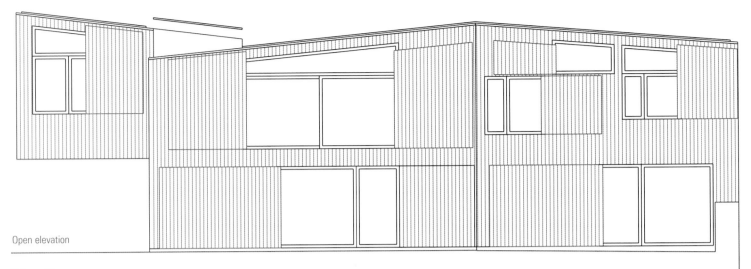

Open elevation

© Eugeni Pons

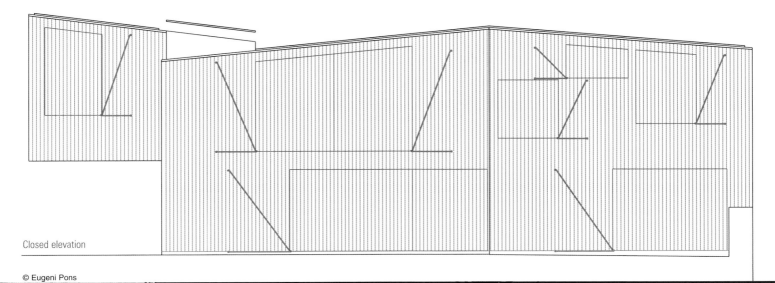

Closed elevation

© Eugeni Pons

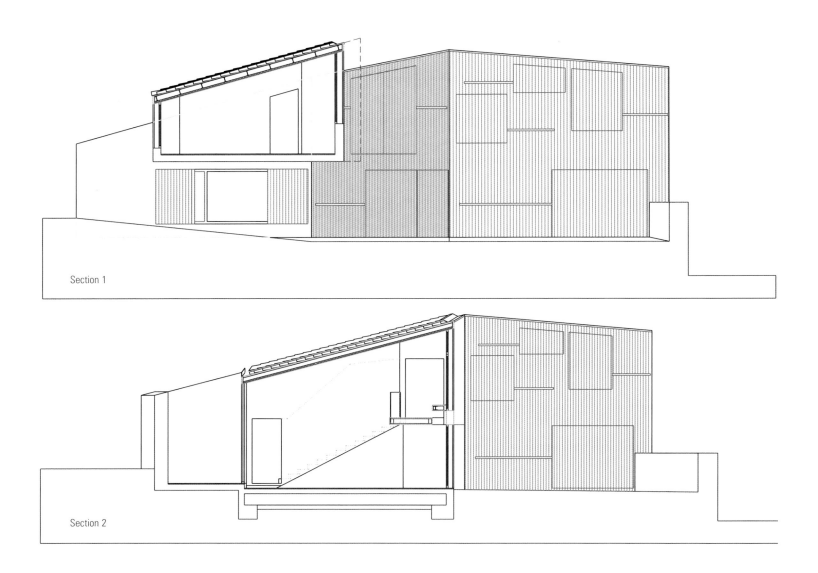

Section 1

Section 2

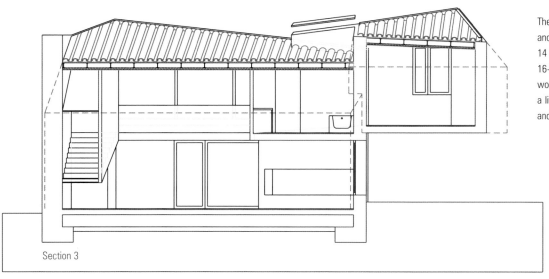

Section 3

The shutters are thus supported at two points and balanced by a third. A prototype measuring 14 square inches (35 sq cm) in surface area with 16-inch-long (40 cm) arms was perfected in the workshop. Having achieved satisfactory results, a life-sized model that multiplied the size by 20 and the arm by 4 was put to the test.

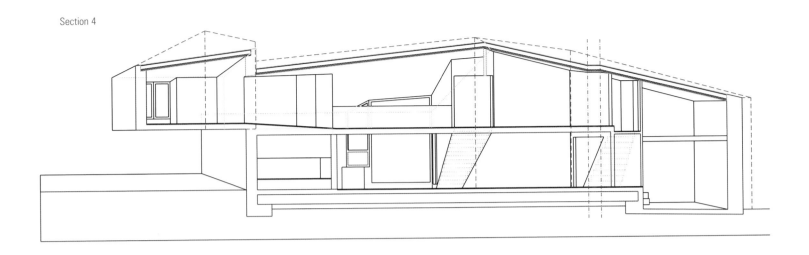

© Eugeni Pons

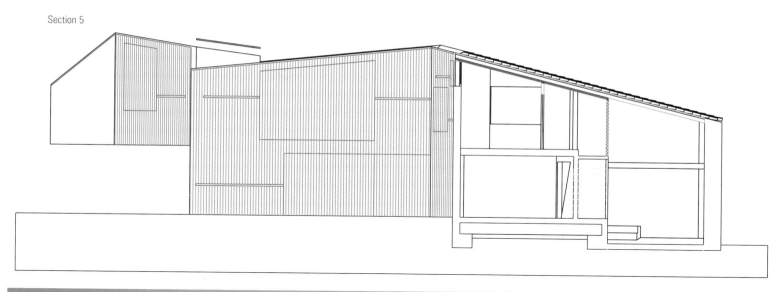

© Eugeni Pons

Construction detail

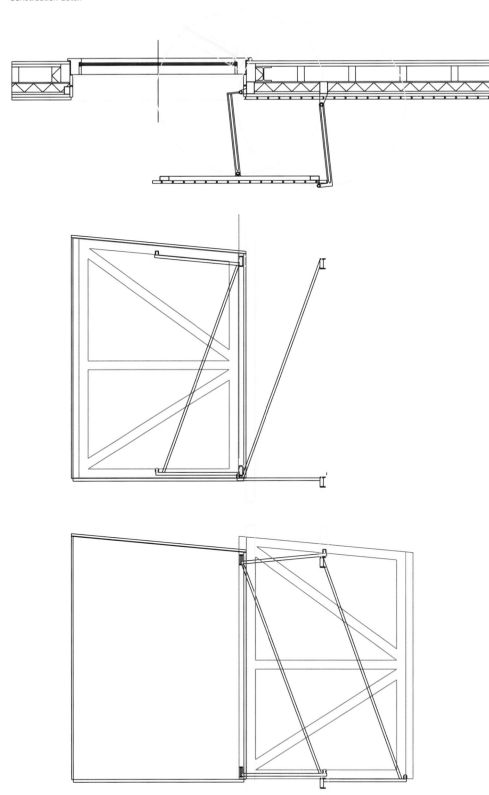

Fink + Jocher

Villa B

Photographs: Simone Rosenberg

Starnberger See, Germany

The building on the west bank of Starnberg Lake is characterized by an amalgam of farming properties and villas dating from the 19th century due to the proximity of the city of Munich. The house seeks to stage views of the changing atmospheres of the adjacent park and lake. This staging takes place on the upper floor, where the atmosphere of the park infuses the bedrooms with a life-filled, ever-changing landscape. The tectonic differences are thereby done away with in favor of tranquility and spatial continuity. This villa is an exercise in blurring the boundary between the rural and the urban, between the surprising and the known.

The most important rooms of the house are located on the upper floor, the only place in the house that truly captures the splendid views of Starnberg Lake. To the east is a cantilevered bedroom that receives natural light on three sides and enjoys a stunning view of the rural park and lake. The individual bedrooms have been placed on the opposite side, facing south. These are accessed via a hallway and are clearly arranged in a hierarchy of intimacy.

As opposed to the original plan, the ample glazing on the exterior skin eventually led to the decision to use a wood structure as the most appropriate construction method in this case. Thus, a series of individual decisions (perforation of the exterior, exposing of the bedrooms) determined the most convenient mode of construction. The highly insulated walls consist of a solid wood for construction (KVH), ecological insulation of cellulose fiber (8.66 in. - 22 cm.) and three-layer plates mounted on the exterior. The roof of the ground floor is composed of thick wooden elements (4.72 in. - 12 cm.) while the upper floor is clad in KVH insulated with 9.84 inch (25cm) cellulose fiber and an extensive roof terrace. In addition to good thermal insulation, particular attention was given to providing quality acoustic insulation for the interior. The panes of glass along the walls also play their part in support and reinforcement. Thanks to the extensive use of boarding on the exterior, the house achieves its aspect as an expression of its construction.

The desire for maximum opening of the bedrooms and the search for a homogenous exterior aspect led to the choice of wood, painted black with a certain degree of brown pigment, both as a load-bearing material and as cladding.

The underlying aim of the program was to stage views of the changing atmosphere of the adjacent park and lake. This staging takes place on the upper floor, where the atmosphere of the park infuses the bedrooms with a life-filled, ever-shifting landscape.

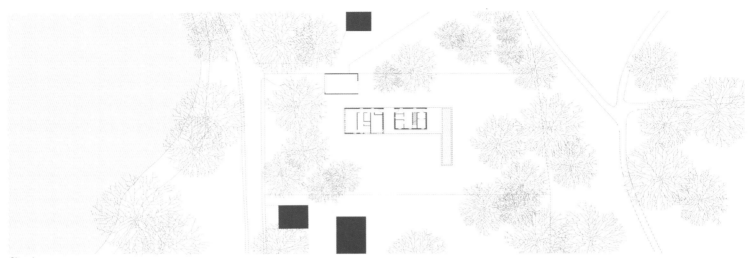

Site plan

South elevation

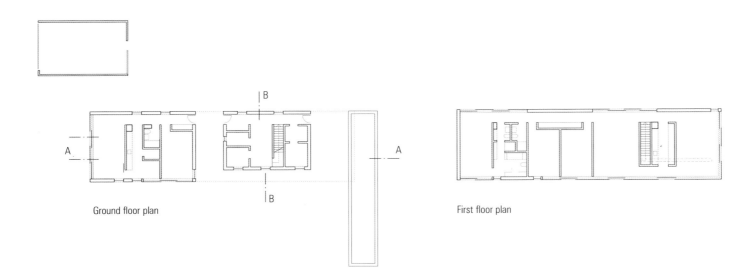

Ground floor plan

First floor plan

The underlying aim of the program was to stage views of the changing atmosphere of the adjacent park and lake. This staging takes place on the upper floor, where the atmosphere of the park infuses the bedrooms with a life-filled, ever-shifting landscape.

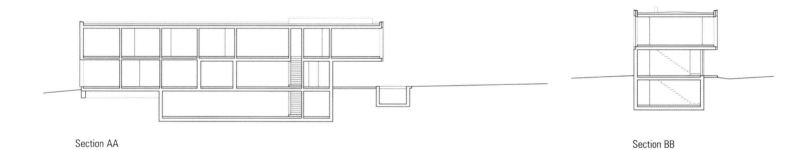

Section AA   Section BB

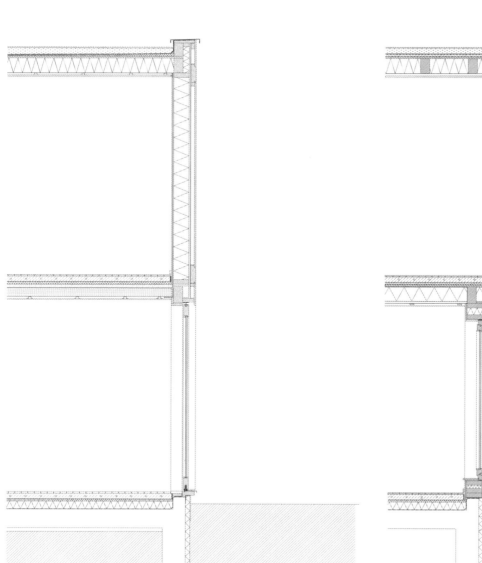

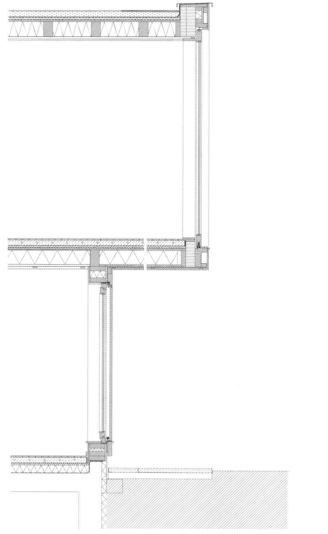

74

Carmen Moreno Álvarez

House in Granada

Photographs: Fernando Alda

Obéilar, Granada, Spain

The house grows outward from a swimming pool set on a platform facing the mountain range and a grove of olive trees. Inspired by the panoramic views, this pool is unusually elongated in form; it has been dug into the terrain following the hill's downward slope toward the valley. Stretching away from a large, wide window as if it were a mirror, its centralized placement helps organize the spaces of which the house is composed. Furthermore, its shimmering surface creates different sensations with the changing light throughout the day and the succession of seasons. On sunny days, it becomes a carpet of light, while going dark and deep on cloudy days, transforming the atmosphere of the spaces around it with its alterations in brightness. The placement and shape of the pool are also related to movement: a person swimming in it toward the horizon has the strangest feeling of being suspended amongst the treetops. Outside the pool, on the other hand, a ramp connects the main platform with another tree-lined walkway just below, these two vantage points being associated with two landscapes: one of distant views and a newly created vista of nearby trees.

Each room enjoys its own distinct views, as if the house had been spun on its axis in an attempt to capture the best of the surrounding landscape: the living room faces the city, the kitchen is oriented toward the Obéilar mountain range, the main bedroom toward the plain and another bedroom has a privileged vantage point of the nearby olive grove.

This layout, so closely connected to the surrounding terrain, provokes a constant exchange between interior and exterior. Furthermore, there is no single entrance into the house, but rather the possibility of choosing where to go on the premises.

Two independent bodies separate the rooms designed for day activities - the kitchen and living room - from the bedrooms, which are joined via a hallway and a staircase. In the volume containing the bedrooms the layout enables the children's rooms (on the upper floor) to be set up as an independent apartment, with its own direct access from the exterior, within the parents' house. A small studio/turret serves as a work space.

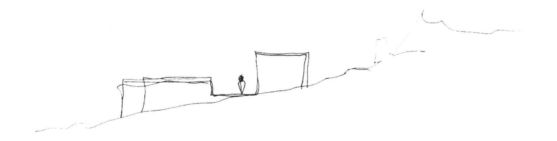

The house grows outward from a swimming pool set on a platform facing the mountain range and a grove of olive trees. Inspired by the panoramic views, this pool is unusually elongated in form; it has been dug into the terrain following the hill's downward slope toward the valley. Stretching away from a large, wide window as if it were a mirror, its centralized placement helps organize the spaces of which the house is composed.

PANORAMIC TERRACE

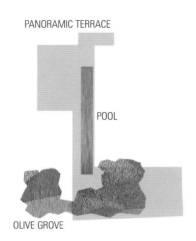

POOL

OLIVE GROVE

DISTRIBUTION SCHEME OF THE INTERIOR SPACES

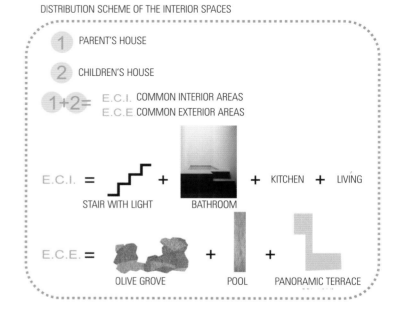

1 PARENT'S HOUSE

2 CHILDREN'S HOUSE

1+2 = E.C.I. COMMON INTERIOR AREAS
       E.C.E. COMMON EXTERIOR AREAS

E.C.I. = STAIR WITH LIGHT + BATHROOM + KITCHEN + LIVING

E.C.E. = OLIVE GROVE + POOL + PANORAMIC TERRACE

PARENT'S HOUSE   CHILDREN'S HOUSE

COMMON EXTERIOR AREAS   COMMON INTERIOR AREAS

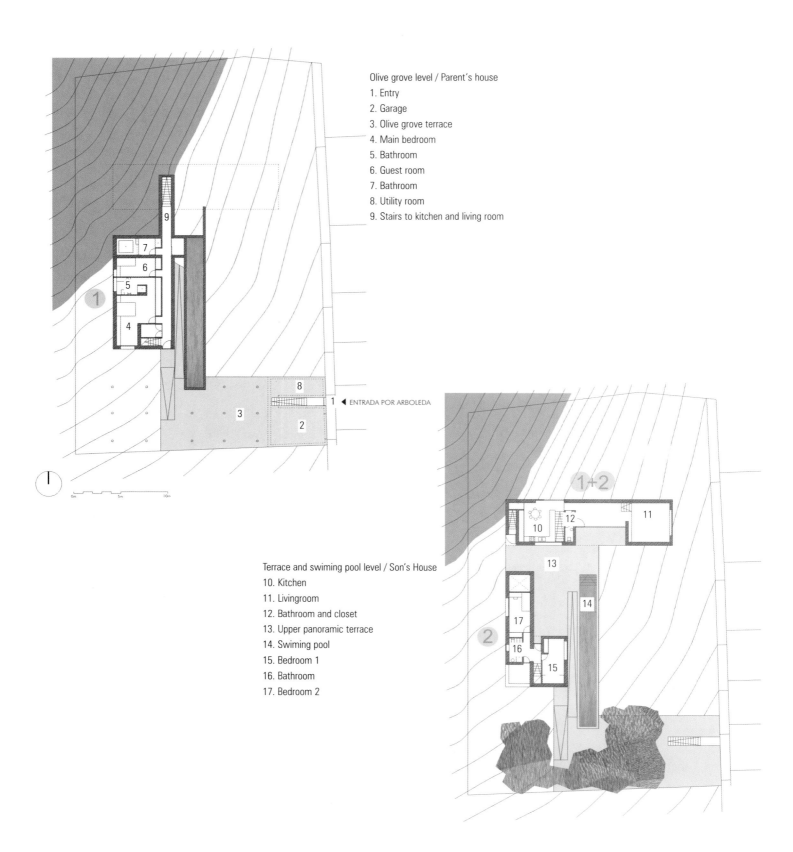

Olive grove level / Parent's house
1. Entry
2. Garage
3. Olive grove terrace
4. Main bedroom
5. Bathroom
6. Guest room
7. Bathroom
8. Utility room
9. Stairs to kitchen and living room

ENTRADA POR ARBOLEDA

Terrace and swiming pool level / Son's House
10. Kitchen
11. Livingroom
12. Bathroom and closet
13. Upper panoramic terrace
14. Swiming pool
15. Bedroom 1
16. Bathroom
17. Bedroom 2

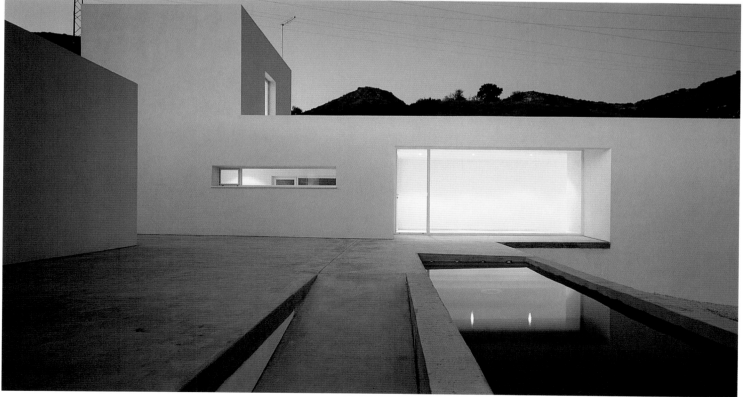

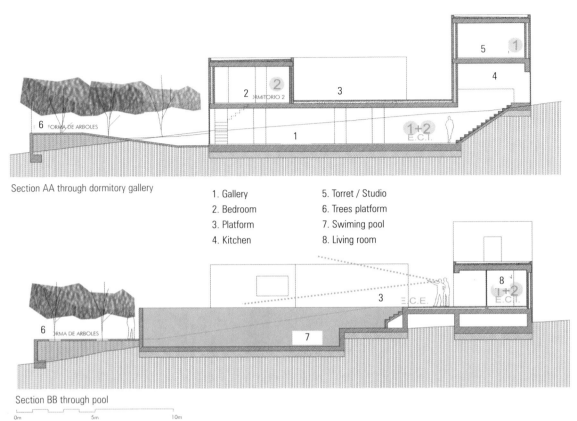

Section AA through dormitory gallery

1. Gallery
2. Bedroom
3. Platform
4. Kitchen
5. Torret / Studio
6. Trees platform
7. Swiming pool
8. Living room

Section BB through pool

0m   5m   10m

Kohki Hiranuma / Hs Workshop - Asia

Time & Space House

Photographs: Syuichi Aida

Osaka, Japan

The site is set two meters lower than an adjacent promenade, and tightly hemmed in by aged houses. These existing characteristics were taken into account when custom designing this house for a young single woman. In ensuring comfort and a sense of openness while bearing in mind the future changes in lifestyle of its single occupant, the dwelling has been designed to outrun time and future generations.

To begin with, a rectangular volume of reinforced concrete and steel was placed along the length of the site. A two-meter wide path owned by the client, yet used by the neighbors, crosses the site and culminates in a parking garage owned by the client's parents. This feature became a necessary part of the design process, as the west portion of the ground floor would be set above the parking spaces and thus had to meet very specific height requirements to allow for vehicle clearance below.

A central courtyard, bound by the east and west volumes, has been created as a natural zone for the occupant's exclusive use. This courtyard also creates an abstracted merging of interior and exterior, the end result being an expanded perception of non-measurable space.

The dwelling itself is a simple, broad space, ingeniously formed by vertical and sequential relations. With only the lightest of touches, a wealth of space has been achieved.

The first floor corridor connects two entirely distinct volumes and sits like a blank box above the south-side walkway. The living room is set higher than the dining room and is partly cantilevered to account for the parking garage to the west, with the connecting corridor adjusted in the middle to make up for these changes in level.

The interior is simple and flexible enough to change with time: the walls and ceilings are exposed concrete with a limited use of gypsum board. The outer wall is also exposed concrete with a water repellant coat and steel fittings. The roof features eight layers of bituminous membrane waterproofing.

Overall, the program is an exercise in how sequential space is created and how it reacts to its surroundings when it has been reduced to a single occupant.

In ensuring comfort and a sense of openness while bearing in mind the future changes in lifestyle, the dwelling has been designed to out-run time and future generations. Overall, the program is an exercise in how sequential space is created and how it reacts to its surroundings when it has been reduced to a single occupant.

construct a ....?

The time ran out very fast.

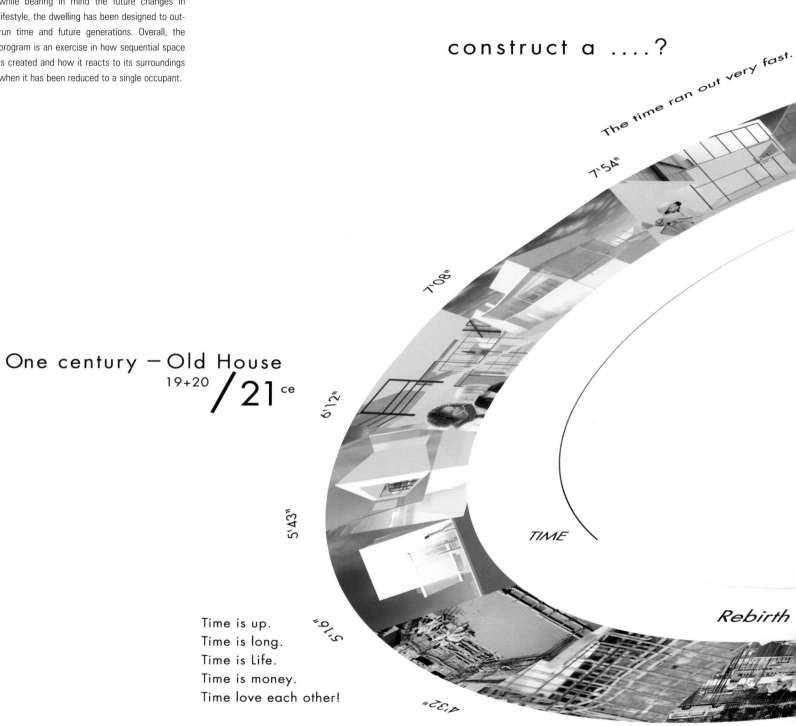

7'54"

7'08"

6'12"

One century — Old House
19+20 /21 ce

5'43"

5'16"

4'32"

4'13"

TIME

Rebirth

Time is up.
Time is long.
Time is Life.
Time is money.
Time love each other!

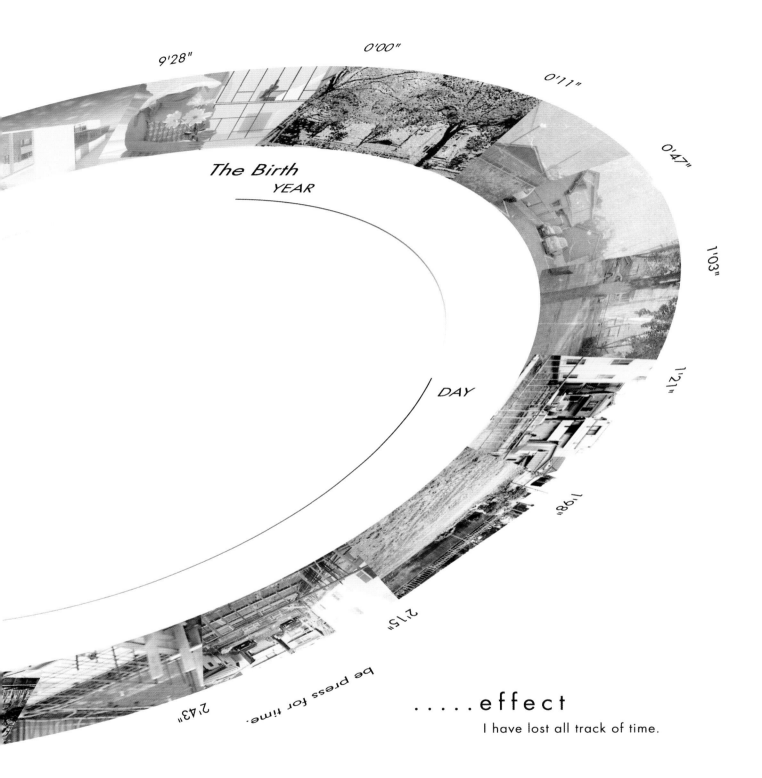

9'28"

0'00"

0'11"

0'47"

1'03"

1'21"

1'58"

2'15"

2'43"

The Birth
YEAR

DAY

be press for time.

.....effect

I have lost all track of time.

Time diagram

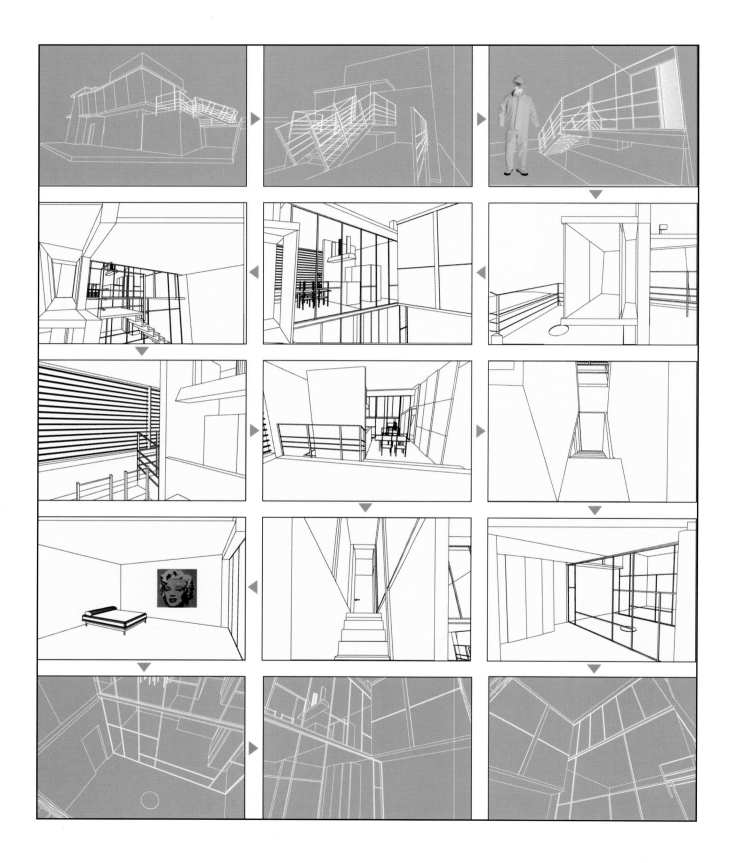

course

volume couse

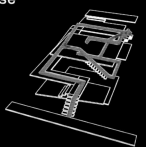
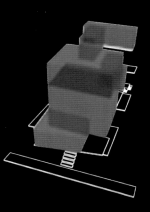
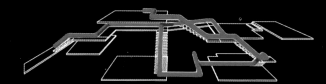
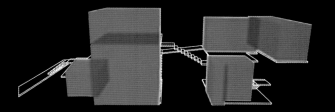
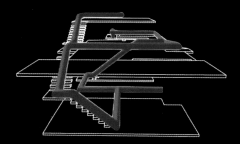
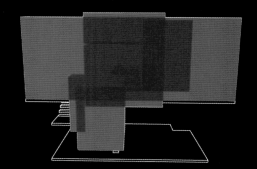
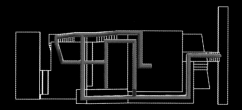
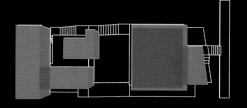

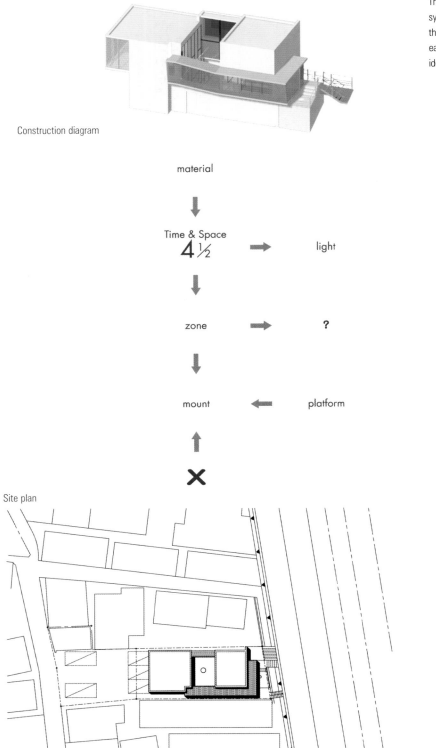

Construction diagram

The word "mount" has been nagging my mind as a system that connects inside space. It is an object that is different from objects often seen in outer areas such as plantations and so on. Somehow the idea may be connected to the project.

material

Time & Space
$4\frac{1}{2}$ ➡ light

zone ➡ ?

mount ⬅ platform

✕

Site plan

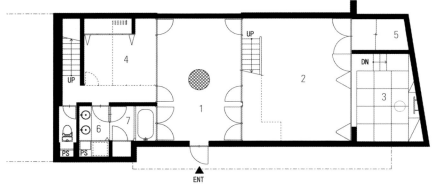

Ground floor plan

1. Courtyard (lightwell)
2. Studio
3. Japanese-styleroom
4. Guestroom
5. Storage
6. Lavatory
7. Bathroom
8. Void (outside)
9. Void (inside)
10. Living room / Kitchen
11. Bedroom
12. Terrace
13. Entrance
14. Garage

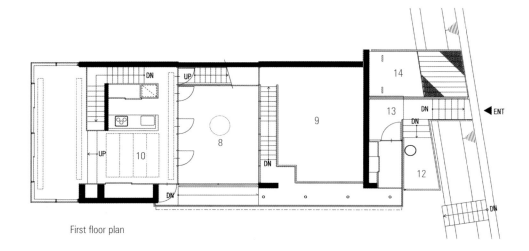

First floor plan

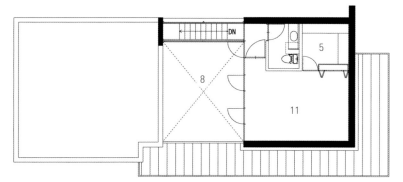

Second floor plan

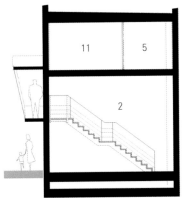

Cross section

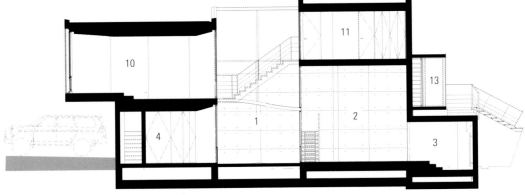

Longitudinal section

Propeller Z

DBL House

Photographs: Margherita Spliuttini

Vienna, Austria

Located on the western outskirts of Vienna, the site of DBL House measures roughly 5382 sq ft (500 sq m), with an allowable footprint limited to 947 sq ft (88 sq m) by building bylaws. The program called for two individual units of approximately 1076 sq ft (100 sq m) each, forcing the structure to expand to the very limits of the maximum volume made possible by the building code.

The allocation of space between the two units, which are occupied by two sisters, was developed in a process in which both occupants were given the possibility to choose from a variety of parameters, such as orientation, lighting, access to the garden, privacy, transparency etc. The evaluation of this process resulted in two markedly different profiles for the units. The slightly smaller one was to be rather closed, but with connection to the south facing street, the larger one was to be transparent and open, with direct access to the garden.

Unit one is organized as a compact volume, the main areas being connected by split-level circulation with a ramp connecting the topmost sleeping box with the lower areas. The whole unit is constructed as a rigid concrete box, which, as a whole is raised above the ground, resting only on the concrete staircase and on three thin steel struts. It thus liberates the ground, forming a roof under which the second unit is located.

With all the necessary structure provided by the first unit, the second is an open space, which is enclosed with glass or light marine plywood walls with a glass strip separating the two units along the whole perimeter. The interior flooring in both units is a combination of hardwood parquet and epoxy resin.

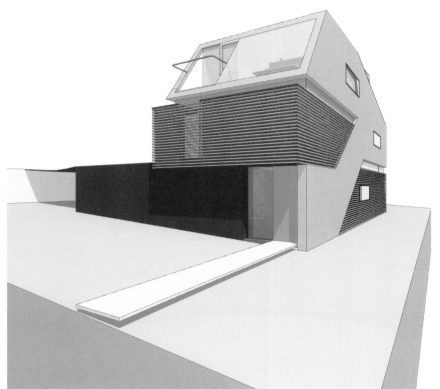

Unit one is organized as a compact volume, the main areas being connected by split-level circulation with a ramp connecting the topmost sleeping box with the lower areas. With all the necessary structure provided by the first unit, the second is an open space, which is enclosed with glass.

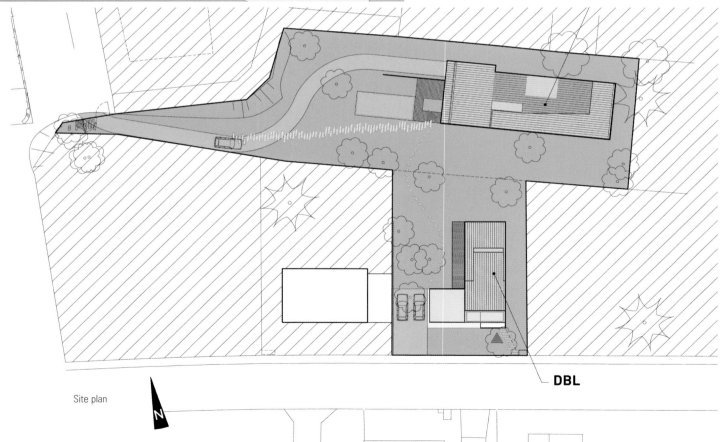

DBL

Site plan

N

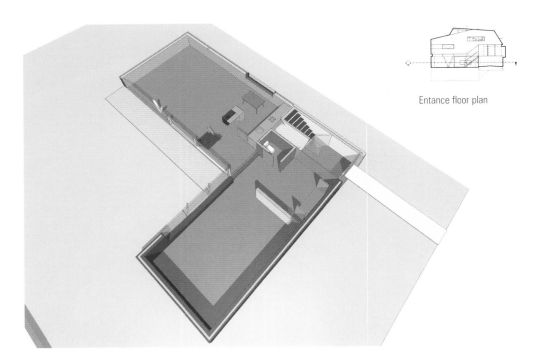

Entance floor plan

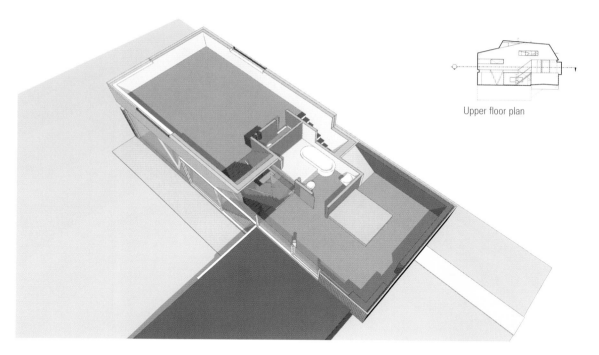

Upper floor plan

111

Jaume Bach

4C House

Photographs: Lluís Casals
Structure: Robert Brufau i Associats

Barcelona, Spain

A couple of houses with a garden dating from around the 1930s had to be turned into a modern urban home. It was deemed necessary to maintain the built perimeter of the buildings since they were located at the back of the small plot; in this way, the sunny, original garden, which was raised above the access street, was able to be conserved. A garage sitting at the level of the street and basement serves as the entrance to the ground floor and garden.

The project was not approached using sophisticated solutions but rather with a sensible use of technology. Even so, there were no special technical details except in the difficulty of execution and in improving the main facades, which were formed by a single plane of solid brick with a lime washed finished on the exterior and plaster on the interior. Once the new openings and voids were adapted, a ventilated façade was designed which contained two layers and the necessary insulation, giving a new exterior image while at the same time ensuring current technology.

To carry this out, the architects custom-designed an earthenware piece supported by stainless steel clamps affixing it to the existing brick. The clamps are hidden, being supported by a series of laterally-placed rods. These clamps can be affixed directly to the wall or, alternately, to vertical fillets wherever there is a need to separate the piece from the wall in order to place sliding panels on some of the balconies.

The doorjambs, ledges and lintels of the openings are 6-millimeter-thick boxes of galvanized sheet metal.

Certain characteristics of the design of the facades influenced the custom-made pieces, which consist of a thin (4 cm) earthenware element with an air chamber cooked at 1200°C. This material was chosen for its structural and visual quality as well as for its inevitable warping, which would distinguish it from the cold perfection of similar cladding materials. The design was approached from a precise laying out of the volumes - a precision which is nonetheless enriched by irregularity.

Site plan

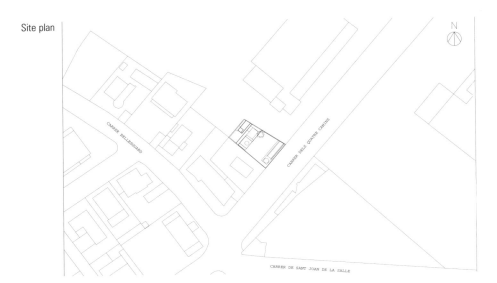

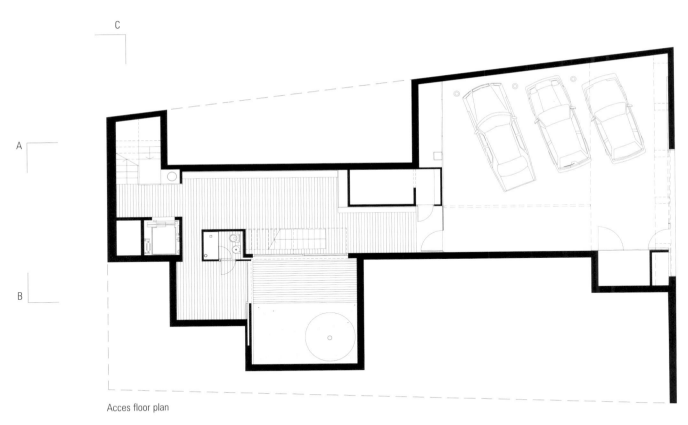

Acces floor plan

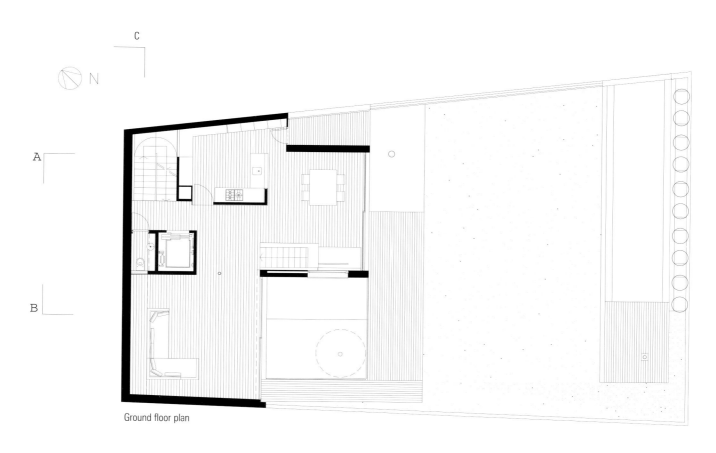

C

N

A

B

Ground floor plan

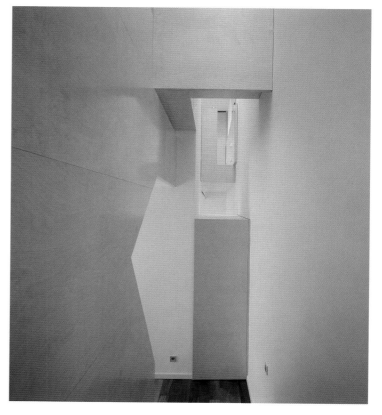

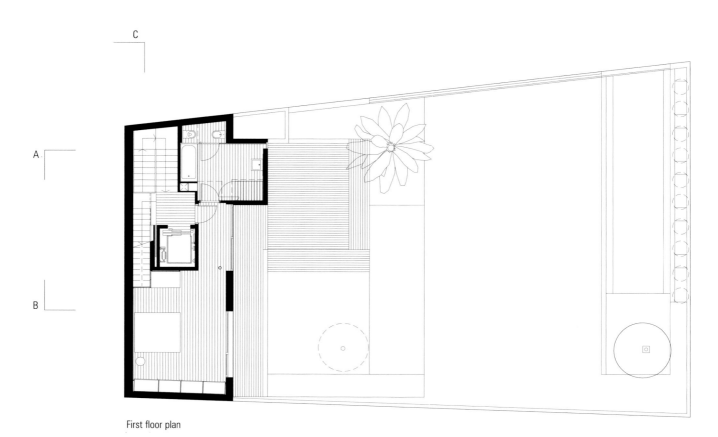

First floor plan

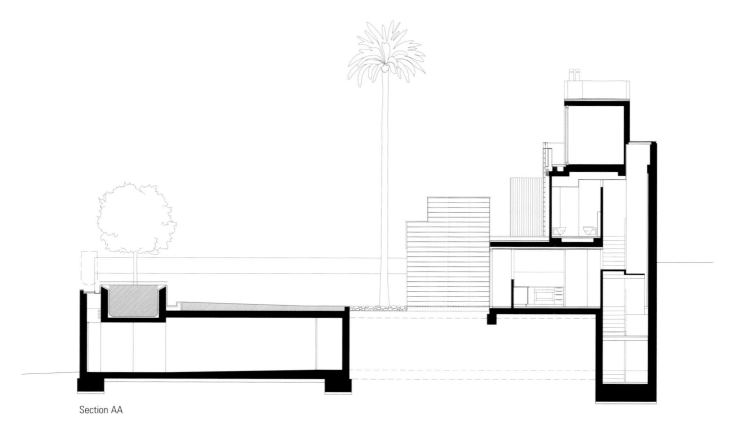

Section AA

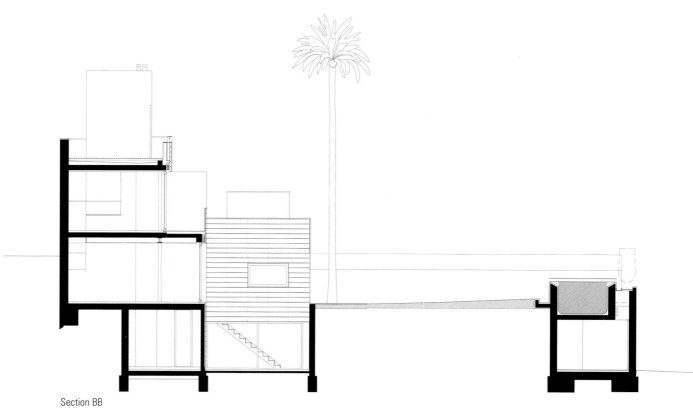

Section BB

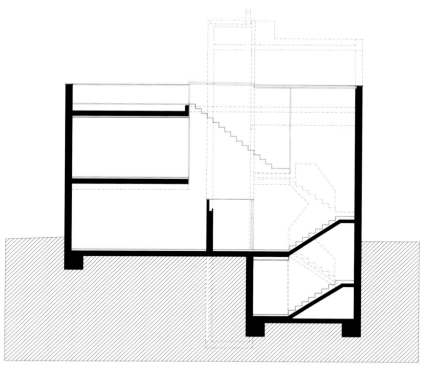

Section CC

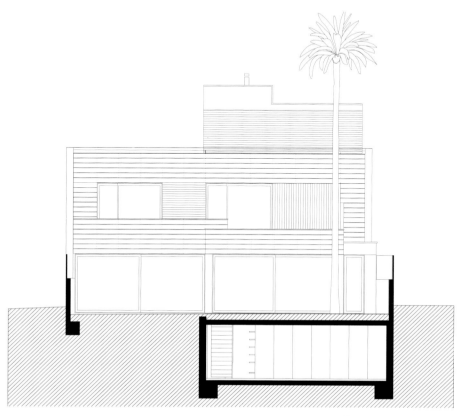

Garden elevation

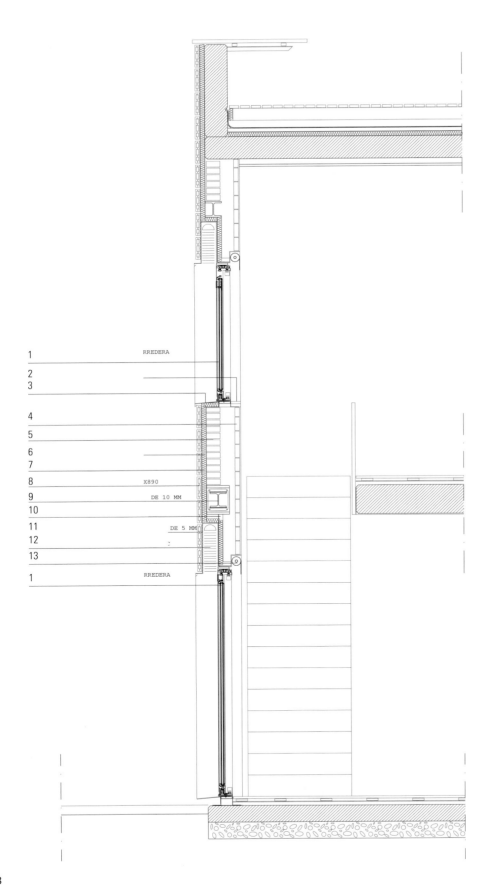

Constructive section
1. Double sliding door, aluminum
2. Wooden lintel, 20 mm
3. Folded aluminum sheet
4. 4 cm thick interior brick lining
5. Structural hollow brick wall
6. Aluminum tubing
7. Spray-on insulation
8. Stonewore element
9. HEB 140 with 10 mm flanges
10. Structural T 40
11. Galvanized steel pierced sheeting 5 mm
12. Gradhermetic shutter, type: Metalunic
13. Retractable curtain

1   RREDERA
2
3
4
5
6
7
8   X890
9   DE 10 MM
10
11   DE 5 MM
12
13
1   RREDERA

Procter:Rihl

Slice House

Photographs: Marcelo Nunes, Sue Barr

Porto Alegre, Brasil

The Slice House project was selected to represent Brazil in the IV Latin American Architecture Biennale in October 2004 in Peru. The house makes a series of references to modern Brazilian architecture as well as adding a new element with its complex prismatic geometry, which generates a series of spatial illusions in the interior spaces. The project is placed on a site measuring 12.14 feet in width and 126.31 feet in length (3.7 m X 38.5 m). Having been vacant for more than 20 years, it had already gone to auction 3 times without any interest whatsoever. The present client was the only one to put in an offer on the 4th auction, as the general bidders could not see the potential.

The project that was eventually decided upon for the renovation uses prismatic geometry with flush details, which demands more careful detailing and site supervision. Remodeling in 3D allowed adjustments to ensure accuracy and precision of delivered components with final sizing on site. Windows, metalwork, and cabinetwork were assembled to fit on-site. These elements were crafted precisely, in contrast to the intentionally rough concrete surfaces.

Wood-formed cast concrete was preferred since it is a local tradition, and pre-cast concrete or metal formwork is not generally available for this size of a project. The wood formwork was built in situ with a plank pattern emphasizing wood grain, accidental texture pattern, and imperfections. The ceilings were cast at a slope angle of 10 degrees, a familiar technique in the Brazilian building process. The terrace and swimming pool employ an in situ technology of resin and fiberglass coatings applied on site after the concrete cured completely.

Probably the best feature of the house is the crafted metal work. The 22.97-foot-long (7 m) kitchen counter is a continuous steel slab with 6.56-foot (2 m) cantilevered tables floating off of both ends at the dining and courtyard sides. The thick steel plate folds up transitionally between the lower dining height and higher work counter. The steel work surface is coated with avocado-colored, two-part catalyzed laboratory paint providing an extremely hard finish. The stair features a .31 inch (8 mm) steel plate accordion folded and welded in sections onto the undercarriage beam plates. Because the stair is a "U" shape with offset forces, the engineers were able to design thinner and lighter balustrade details than normal.

Wood-formed cast concrete was preferred since it is a local tradition, and pre-cast concrete or metal formwork is not generally available for this size of a project. The wood formwork was built in situ with a plank pattern emphasizing wood grain, accidental texture pattern, and imperfections.

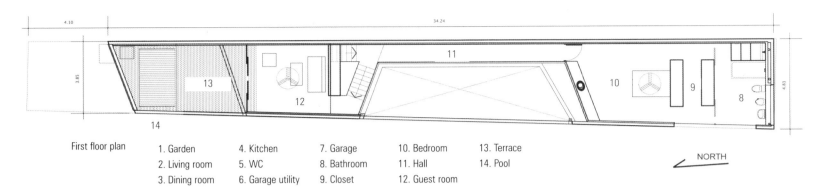

First floor plan

1. Garden	4. Kitchen	7. Garage	10. Bedroom	13. Terrace
2. Living room	5. WC	8. Bathroom	11. Hall	14. Pool
3. Dining room	6. Garage utility	9. Closet	12. Guest room	

NORTH

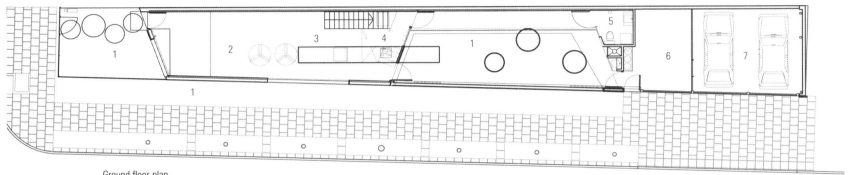

Ground floor plan

© Marcelo Nunes

The ceilings were cast at a slope angle of 10 degrees, a familiar technique in the Brazilian building process. The terrace and swimming pool employ an in situ technology of resin and fiberglass coatings applied on site after the concrete cured completely.

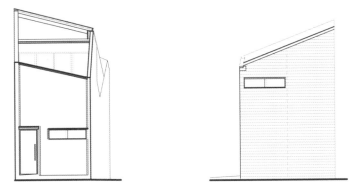

North elelvation

South elelvation

© Marcelo Nunes

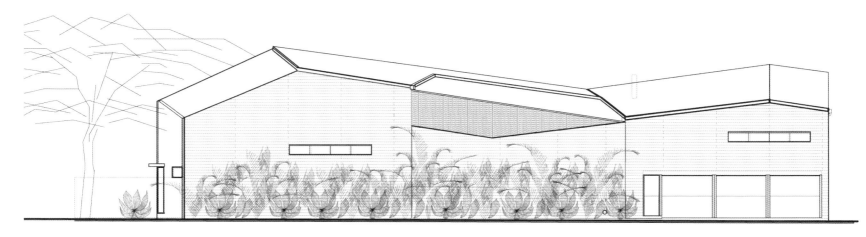

West elelvation

© Marcelo Nunes

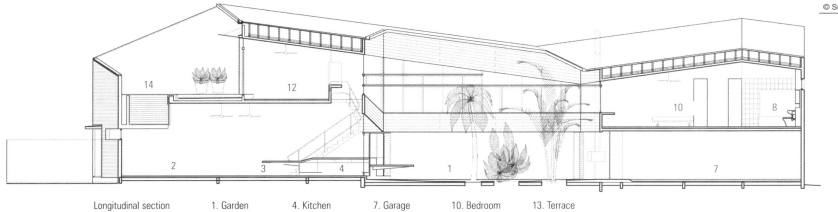

Longitudinal section	1. Garden	4. Kitchen	7. Garage	10. Bedroom	13. Terrace
	2. Living room	5. WC	8. Bathroom	11. Hall	14. Pool
	3. Dining room	6. Garage utility	9. Closet	12. Guest room	

Jarmund/Vigsnæs

Villa Flindt

Photographs: Nils Petter Dale

Nesodden, Norway

Villa Flindt Vraalsen is a coastal property located on the peninsula of Nesodden, to the south of Oslo. The easiest route to this remote spot is via boat from the city center.

Set on a wild, rocky slope, the site's immediate natural surroundings combined with the far off views of Oslo (views which are particularly spectacular at night) make for an especially unique and aesthetically pleasing setting.

Furthermore, the conflicting desires to capture the greatest amount of sunlight (to the south) on the one hand and optimal views on the other (to the west as well as to the north) create an interesting tension in the project which has in fact become its guiding theme.

In the end, the living spaces were placed on the top floor, oriented to the north, where nighttime views are especially attractive. The kitchen and dining room, which open onto a spacious terrace, are also located here.

The lower floor houses the entrance and the bedrooms, which face more immediate views of the area's rugged nature.

The concrete structure of the ground floor was poured in situ. It is clad in vertical wooden formwork, which precisely conforms to the natural granite rock contour of the side. All additional cladding is in Siberian larch wood.

Site plan

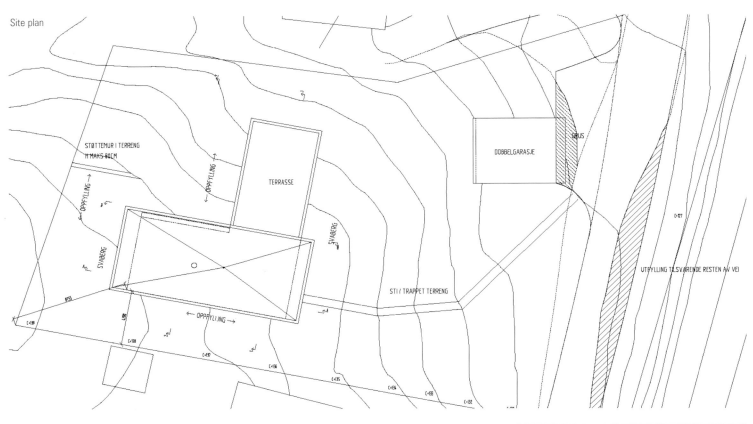

STØTTEMUR I TERRENG
H MAKS 80CM

OPPFYLLING

OPPFYLLING

TERRASSE

SVABERG

SVABERG

DOBBELGARASJE

GRUS

C+127

UTFYLLING TILSVARENDE RESTEN AV VEI

STI / TRAPPET TERRENG

OPPFYLLING

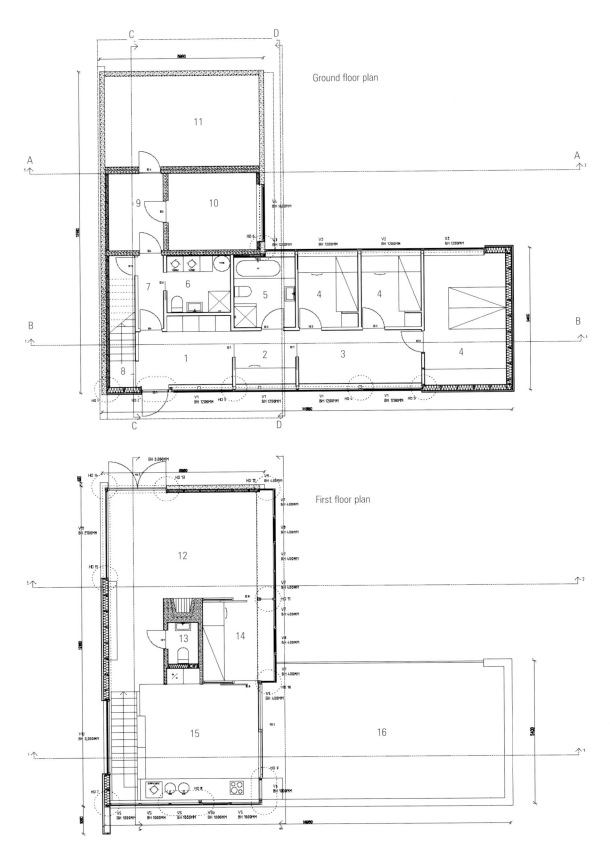

Ground floor plan

First floor plan

1. Entrance
2. Studio
3. Playroom
4. Bedroom
5. Bathroom
6. Laundry
7. Hall
8. Stair
9. Storeroom
10. Storeroom / Guestroom
11. Utility room
12. Living room
13. WC
14. Guestroom / Studio
15. Kitchen
16. Terrace

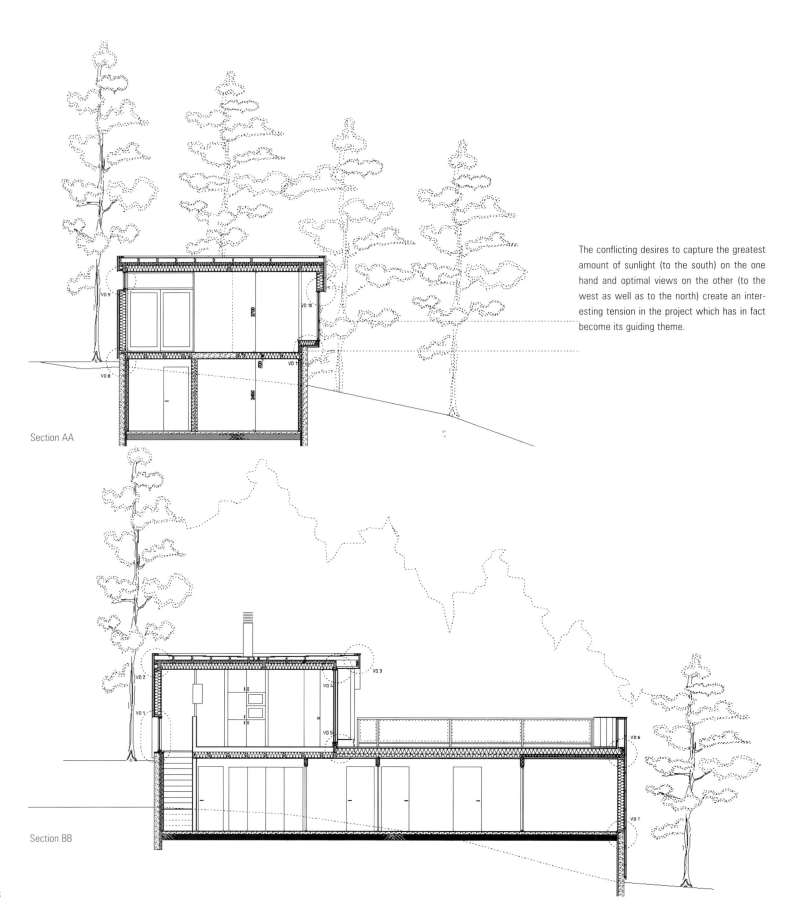

Section AA

The conflicting desires to capture the greatest amount of sunlight (to the south) on the one hand and optimal views on the other (to the west as well as to the north) create an interesting tension in the project which has in fact become its guiding theme.

Section BB

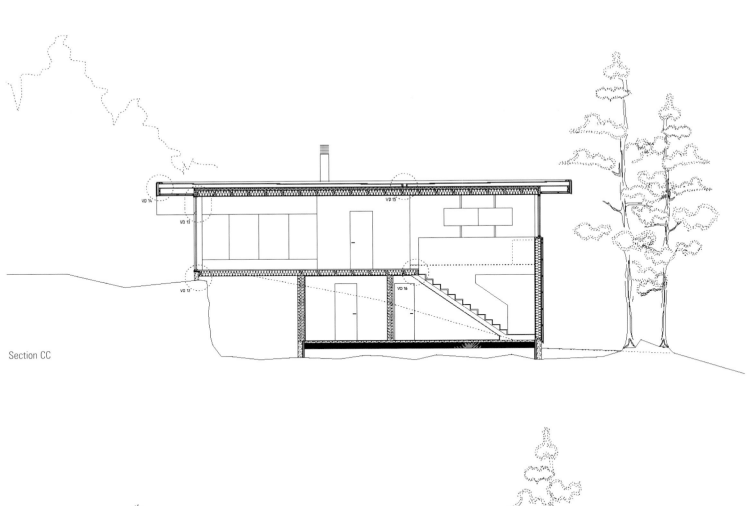

Section CC

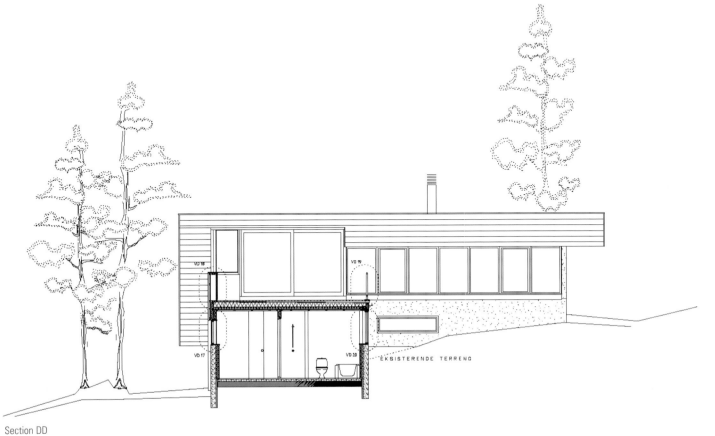

EKSISTERENDE TERRENG

Section DD

Hiroaki Ohtani

Layer House

Photographs: Kouji Okamoto

Kobe, Japan

The architect chose a very small plot measuring only 355.21 sq ft (33 sq m) in the heart of Kobe city for his family home. The challenge (and central design theme) was to create as spacious and rich an indoor space as possible on such a tiny plot bounded by existing buildings at the back and sides. Since such restraints also meant that large construction equipment could not be used, the architect came up with a new construction method, in which pre-stressed concrete strips were manually stacked to form the walls; the construction is thus entirely devoid of vertical members.

Being custom designed by the eventual inhabitants of the home, the design scheme incorporates their own very personal preferences and philosophies. For example, they wanted a house that would be open toward the city while at the same time maintaining a sense of privacy. Hence, the front façade of the house is largely glazed, yet the floors have been placed above or below the level of the street to eliminate direct sight lines.

In spite of the site's highly reduced proportions, the architect made the unconventional decision to set the façade back from the edge of the plot in order to make room to plant a tall tree just outside the windows of the front façade. Inside, care has been taken to ensure fluidity - not a sin-gle space has stagnant air. This has been achieved, in part, through the lack of partitions on each floor. This also creates a greater sense of space, as do the continuous connections between the floors; the cantilevered steps of these gentle flights of stairs become pieces of furniture in the rooms where they originate.

The decision to include very little storage space was deliberate - this way the occupants are immediately faced with messes and are thereby prompted to keep the spaces tidy. The few storage spaces and bookshelves that have been deemed necessary are all elevated so that every corner of the floor surface is visible, thus ensuring greater visual spaciousness.

The pervading sense of order in this house is heightened by the effective concealing of light switches and receptacles, such as, for example, between the pre-cast wall elements. None of the lighting fixtures and shelves, even those that have been inserted into the voids in the walls, is fixed; they can all be quickly and easily relocated.

The pre-cast concrete wall elements are not completely uniform in size and shape and many of them have minor cracks or are chipped. These irregularities were embraced as an important part of the overall look of the home; the architect views them as examples of "beautiful variety".

Since large construction equipment could not be used, the architect came up with a new construction method, in which pre-stressed concrete strips were manually stacked to form the walls. Pre-cast concrete wall elements are not completely uniform in size and shape and many of them have minor cracks or are chipped. These irregularities were embraced as an important part of the overall look of the home; the architect views them as examples of "beautiful variety".

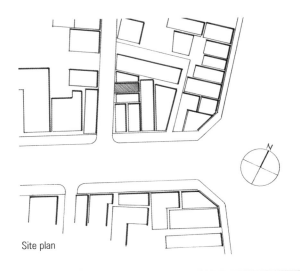

Site plan

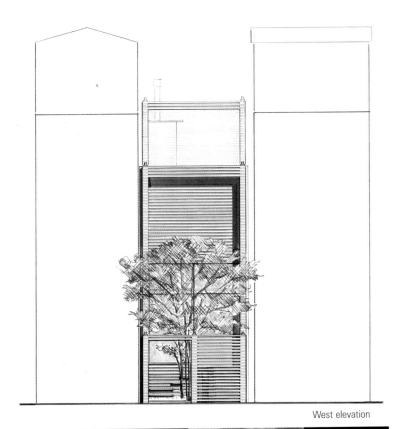

West elevation

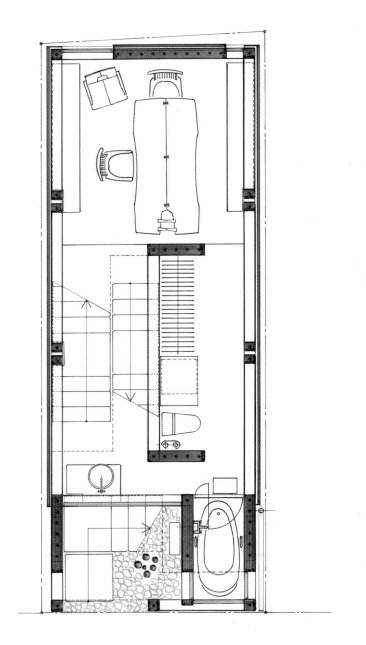

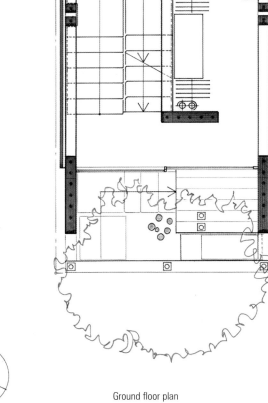

Basement floor plan

Ground floor plan

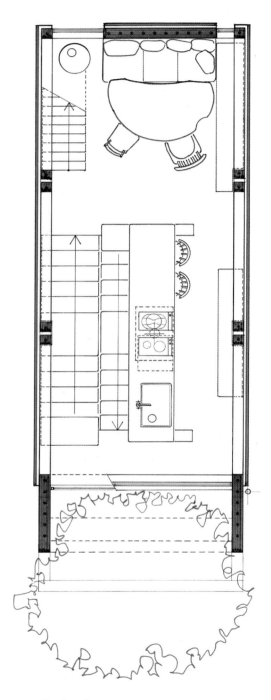

First floor plan

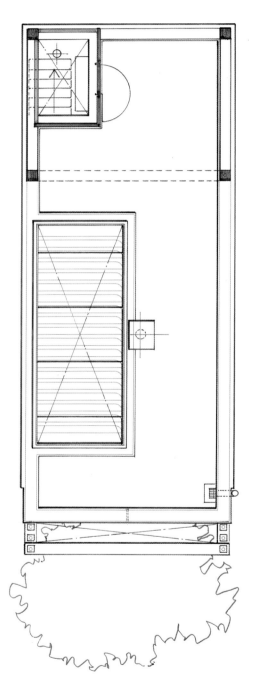

Roof plan

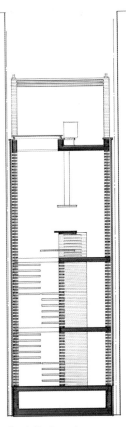

South North section

East West section